Buzz to the Rescue!

Published by Scholastic Inc., *Publishers since 1920*. SCHOLASTIC and associated logos
are trademarks and/or registered trademarks of Scholastic Inc. All rights reserved.

The publisher does not have any control over and does not assume
any responsibility for author or third-party websites or their content.

This book is a work of fiction. Names, characters, places, and incidents are either the product of the
author's imagination or are used fictitiously, and any resemblance to actual persons, living or dead,
business establishments, events, or locales is entirely coincidental.

ISBN: 978-1-338-57288-9

10 9 8 7 6 5 4 3 2 1   19 20 21 22 23

Printed in Malaysia   106

First printing, 2019

Book design by Marissa Asuncion

Scholastic Inc.

One of Andy's toys
is lost outside.

Woody is **up** in Andy's room,
but he still has to help his friend.

Outside, Woody
finds the lost toy.
But a man picks **up** Woody.
He puts Woody in his bag
and **runs** off.
Woody is in **trouble**!

Buzz sees the man
take Woody.
Buzz wants to help.
He **jumps** out the window.
He **runs** after the man.

Buzz **rushes** to help Woody.
But he is too late!

The car zooms away.
Woody is **stuck**!

Buzz comes **up** with a plan.
It is very dangerous,
but the toys **must** save Woody!

Buzz and the other toys **jump** in a **truck.** They drive to where Woody is trapped.

The toys make their way
into the building.
They find Woody.
The toys pull Woody
to safety.

The toys **bust** out!
Woody is saved!
Well done, Buzz.